Help Me With My Teenager!
A Step-by-step Guide For Parents That Works

Christina Botto

2006

Help Me With My Teenager!

Help Me With My Teenager! A step-by-step guide for parents that works is intended to be educational and in no way a substitute for specific advice from a mental health professional. The author and publisher expressly disclaim responsibility for any negative effects directly or indirectly attributable to the use or application of any information contained in this book.

No part of this book may be reproduced or transmitted in any form or by any means, electronic or mechanical, including photocopying, recording, or by any other information storage and retrieval system, without permission in writing from the author.

Copyright © 2006 Christina Botto
Edited by: Margaret D. Beck

All rights reserved.
www.helpwithteenagers.com

ISBN: 1-4196-3704-5

Library of Congress Control Number: 2006904525

To order additional copies, please contact us.
BookSurge, LLC
www.booksurge.com
1-866-308-6235
orders@booksurge.com

Help Me With My Teenager!

Table of Contents

Foreword	ix
CHAPTER I	
The Road Ahead	1
Understanding Your Teenager	3
Accepting Teenage Behavior	6
CHAPTER II	
Connecting With Your Teenager	11
Developing Conversations	15
Listening To Your Teenager	19
CHAPTER III	
Giving Your Teenager Room To Grow	21
Begin With Small Tasks	23
When Parents Try Too Hard	28
CHAPTER IV	
Your Teenager's Friends	33
Freedom—I Have a Driver's License	40
CHAPTER V	
Setting Limits	43
Curfew	47
A Teenagers' Room	50
CHAPTER VI	
Enjoying Your Teenager	53

Foreword

When my older daughter started to display the "typical" teenage behavior, such as arguing with me over anything and ignoring everything I said, I was completely unprepared. If we went food shopping together, I would find myself getting lectured on the products I was buying, why they were disgusting, and how no one was going to eat them. She began questioning why we had to clean the house every week since it was not even dirty. She refused to help when I cleaned; claiming that I could waste all the time I wanted, but there was no way she was going to do so.

Apparently I did not know how to properly do laundry; she asked me not to do her laundry anymore since she would rather do it herself. I also seemed to lack driving skills. I was lectured for going too fast or too slow, taking turns too tight or too wide, should have seen that the light was turning red and slowed down sooner, or should have been able to make it through that light.

As the parent of a teenager, you are already aware that the list of the things we parents do not know how to do is a lot longer than what I have listed, but that would be a book in itself. We find ourselves defending what we do and why. We want to tell our teenager that even if they are convinced that they know better, as long as they live in our house, they better do as we say. The arguments continue, most of the time getting worse to the point where you and your teenager start to avoid one another.

My older daughter and I had a terrible time during her first two years of being a teenager. It was hard for me to accept her changing from a quiet and obedient girl to a person who wanted to make her own decisions. I specifically remember when my daughter was five years old and I took her with me when I went to take an admissions test for a college course. She had brought along her Barbie case to keep her entertained while I was testing. I asked her to please stay in the waiting room while I took the test and to not leave the chair she was in. When I returned 30 minutes later, she was exactly where I had left her, still playing with her Barbies®.

Suddenly, as a teenager, she contradicted me at every opportunity. She would not wear the clothes I bought for her. She did not call me when she returned home from school, claiming she forgot—even though she knew I just wanted to know that she was home and safe. We argued over everything, and there was a lot of tension between us.

A friend of mine recommended taking something my daughter enjoyed having away from her in order to get her to listen to and obey me. Desperate to get my house back in order, I followed my friend's advice. My daughter had a favorite hairbrush and I chose that as the item I would remove. I can still see the fire in my daughter's eyes as I was telling her she would receive it back once she decided to listen to me and my instructions again. Instead of bringing the success I hoped for, it made matters worse. Now my daughter had a reason to be mad at me and she took full advantage of it. She did not miss an opportunity to let me feel it. True hostilities ensued and it seemed that we hated each other.

The reality was my daughter and I did not hate each other,

but we were pulling in opposite directions. She was trying to gain independence, to discover herself. She wanted to take baby-steps towards living an independent life. I was trying to force her back into my five-year-old obedient child. I wanted her to keep following my instructions without questioning my motives or actions. With both of us following different agendas, it was only natural that there were conflicts and we could not work together.

Our disagreements and arguments became so bad that at one point they almost became a physical fight. When we both realized the intensity of our opposition, we were equally shocked. Seeing what had just transpired brought us to a level where reconciliation was possible. We looked at each other for a long time not really knowing where and how to start. We began to talk.

In retrospect, I have to say that my older daughter must have mustered all her guts to speak what was on her mind, risking that I was going to ground her until she was a grandmother. However, the shock that she had almost attacked her mother opened the floodgates of her emotions and she began to speak what was in her heart.

I listened, and picked up some very important points of reference from her flood of words. We sat down a few days later and looked closer at the source of our conflict. My daughter repeated to me her reasons for not following my orders and instructions blindly. Together we began to work on gaining a better understanding of one another. We discussed what we expected from each other and how we both would have to act in order to accommodate each other. I had to come to terms with giving her some independence. We both had to agree on what she would be able to decide and what not.

Since this talk with my older daughter, I have made it a point to listen to as many teenagers as possible. When we went on an outing, I made sure my kids would bring a couple of friends along. I spoke both with their friends and with their friends' parents to see if both sides were facing the same issues as my daughter and me.

Some of the boys and girls, after realizing my interest and understanding of the situation, asked their parents to talk with me. I recall one incident when the mother of a teenage boy came to see me at her son's request. She was wondering what he had done wrong now.

I replied, "Oh, something really bad. He turned into a teenager." That broke the ice, and she stayed a couple of hours, discussing the issues and difficulties she was facing with her teenage son.

Over the past 14 years, I have discussed teenagers with many friends and coworkers. I learned to differentiate between teenage issues that are more personality specific, and those difficulties and problems which are common when raising a teenager. I came to understand the issues with which teenagers are dealing, and I re-learned what it meant to be a teenager.

I naturally understood the parents' point of view. As my popularity and my understanding of teenagers' and parents' issues grew, I have been asked to be a mediator by parents and their teenagers. The more I listened and interacted between teenagers and parents, the more my understanding grew and I learned to relate better to both groups.

By the time my younger daughter started to display teenage traits, I was well prepared. Practicing and applying what I had learned gave me the ability to differentiate between a "smart remark" that should be ignored, and a mumbled comment that really was a cry for help and needed a response.

My younger daughter did not even realize that I was giving her more and more room to develop her individuality or how closely I paid attention to what she was capable of doing and deciding—it was an ongoing, smooth transition. I had learned to be supportive without smothering her. She, and her friends, loved to be with and around me. I was the "cool mom" and my daughter's friends envied her for it.

I am proud to say that my younger daughter's teenager years were the most wonderful times with her so far. I was at her side when she turned from a girl to a young lady, enjoying and experiencing changes and accomplishments step by step. Time flew by, and when she went to college, I realized that a friend was leaving.

A couple of months later she called me late in the night, and we talked for over an hour. When she said something to other people in her dorm-room, she readily explained to me "They are making fun of me because I am talking so long with my *mom*." It was then I realized that I had graduated, too. I had become her friend.

Last summer while listening to my favorite radio station on my way to work, I heard a caller complaining about her teenager. She and the host discussed teenagers and how they drove them crazy. The host and caller compared notes on what teenagers think they know and what they don't know. Finally, both agreed they couldn't wait for their teenager to move out.

"What a shame," I thought, "I wish I could reach out to them and tell both mothers that they are trying to hurry through what could be the most wonderful time with their children. If only I could let them know how to go about to make these years pleasurable for themselves as well as their teenager."

In that moment I was inspired to write this book. So for the lady who called in frustrated over her teenager's behavior, and all parents of teenagers, I will share with you more than 14 years of successfully relating to and interacting with teenagers. In this book, I will address the most common problem areas of a parent teenager relationship. I will explain the standpoint of the teenager in these respective problem areas and give examples on how to handle these various situations.

I want to share my knowledge and give you the tools to parent your teenager successfully. You will be able to give them the support they need. You and your teenager will learn to understand each other and will form a bond that lasts a lifetime. Most importantly, you and your teenager will have fun along the way and enjoy each other's company.

This book will also give you a better understanding of the emotional stages that your teenager faces developing from a child to a young adult. Each chapter gives you the insight what and how your teen feels. This is not theories learned in college—it comes directly from the many teenagers who told me so. I was able to gain their confidence and get them to talk and relate to me—through this book, so will you. You will be pleased to discover how much your teen wants and needs your advice and support.

Each child is unique, so it is not possible to give word-for-word instructions to be used as a script. However, you will find examples of dialog to be adapted to the various situations.

As you read through the chapters, you might be surprised at how simple and logical it all sounds. However, living it every day for at least five years is certainly no easy task. From my experience as a parent who raised two teenagers and some of their friends along the way, and from listening and talking to many parents, I can assure you it is anything but easy.

It is not possible to put into words all the different and opposing emotions that you will have to deal with on your end. Instead of instinctively correcting your son or daughter, you will have to focus on what you want to accomplish and guide yourself and your teenager through the process. Is there someone in your life who truly knows how to push your buttons? When dealing with your teenager, it will help considerably if you can deactivate these buttons first. As the parent, we also carry all the responsibility, and naturally we worry about them. We want to solve their problems ourselves in order to save our teenagers from potential harm, but there are times when we should give them the opportunity to handle the situation themselves.

There will be many times when you feel like you are not making any progress at all or even feel like banging your head against the wall. Sometimes you will get information from and about your teen that you really did not want to know. You will have discussions with your teenager that will make you wonder if you are the parent or his or her friend. Hopefully you will be both.

As you join your son or daughter's journey from childhood to young adult, you have to become your teenager's friend while still being the parent. This dual role naturally will cause emotional conflict. As the parent, you still have to set limits and boundaries for your son or daughter. As their friend, you give them the necessary guidance to move within these boundaries. By watching and observing, you will be able to judge the areas where your teen is capable of making decisions, and the areas where he or she still needs your guidance. Your primary focus throughout your son's or daughter's journey to adulthood is to give the support needed to become independent, successful, and responsible adults.

As a search on the Internet will quickly reveal, teenage suicide is currently the third leading cause of death and, unfortunately, on the rise. Peer pressure is increasing, leaving teens with many issues with which they need guidance. Overwhelmed by the physical and mental changes of adolescence, your teenager needs to have a safe place where he can relax. He also needs someone he can trust, knowing that that person is on his side and ready to help without question whenever he needs it. As much as friends are important in this stage of a teenager's live, only an adult has the necessary experience to provide the safety and security he or she needs.

Your teenager will need your help in developing a sense of direction. They will need your support in learning how to make decisions. They need to learn to trust that you have their welfare at heart and that you are making suggestions that have their best interests at heart. They have to learn how to trust their own decisions in order to grow into confident young adults.

It is a long, hard journey, and at times you will be so frustrated that you consider giving up trying and just let things run. Please believe me when I tell you that the ultimate outcome is worthwhile—you will not regret the times you bit your tongue, held your breath, punched the wall, banged your head, and grinned through clenched teeth.

These are the years that your child needs you and your support the most. On this journey with your teenager, you will experience the most exhilarating joy from every little success and every positive feedback. During these years, your relationship with your child will grow from a parent-child relationship to a friend-friend relationship.

CHAPTER I
The Road Ahead

Between the ages of 13 and 18, your teenager will transform from a child that followed your lead and had everything done for him to a young adult, ready to take on life and live on his own. He will have to decide on what profession he wants to pursue, which college to go to, and what path he will pursue in life.

Where is your teenager today, and where do you want her to be when she graduates high school? Think for a minute about this tremendous change. Reflect on all the various areas in which she will have to gain experience, and the decisions that she will have to learn to make.

Your son or daughter will have to learn everything from washing clothes to earning a living to handling personal relationships. They will have to decide if they will go to college, what their field of study will be, what profession they want to pursue, and which college to go to. They will get a driver's license, and will start going their own way instead of going along with the rest of the family.

During these five years parents have the unique opportunity to give their teenager more and more responsibility and allow them to make more and more decisions about their lives. They need to grow more independent with each day.

As parents, we will be there for them if they fail or make a wrong choice. We need to be careful not to underestimate our teenager and, at the same time, not to ask too much of them too soon, thus discouraging them from making decisions. We need to give them enough space to develop, while standing by to help. We need to encourage and support them, and teach them that what they do will affect their future life.

Understanding Your Teenager

When your child was five years old, you could hold onto their hand and safely lead them everywhere in life. You had this wonderful child who listened to you, followed your instructions with little or no complaining, and never gave you any serious trouble. They enjoyed taking part in family outings, camping trips, and vacations. They were always ready to go out for ice cream, a walk together, or even to the mall with the entire family. Your daughter wanted to help with household chores, do the laundry and cleaning, or look after younger siblings. Your son loved washing the car, mowing the grass, and bringing in the groceries. He was proud to help and be your "little man."

Once these same children reach adolescence, you find yourself begging them to go places with the family. As soon as your teen gets into the car with you, she begins complaining about you or her life, and how miserable everything in her world is. In just a few minutes of being within the same five-foot radius of one another, the two of you are already in an argument.

There may have been times you regretted asking your teen to join you on your daily activities. No matter where you go, or what you do, your teen seems to find something to complain about. You are purchasing the wrong items, the whole trip is "so ridiculous," you are just the worst parent ever, and he hates his life!

Instead of getting frustrated or angry, remember that every teenager does this. Teens everywhere believe their life is just a depressing, revolting state of time and they wish everything from their parents, to their friends, to their clothes, to their body, was different.

You have tried to teach your child right from wrong. You tried to teach him social skills and to be responsible for his actions. You were always able to get along and had so much fun when you went out together, no matter what the activity was. Suddenly and without warning, you have to deal with an obstinate, argumentative and rebellious teenager. No matter what you do or how hard you try, you are unable to connect on any level with your child. You find yourself asking what you did wrong, where did your sweet baby go, and where did this hostile teenager come from?

Your child's world, as he knows it, has ended. When your child entered puberty, an alarm clock went off in his mind, waking him from the comfort of being a child.

Up until now, she had the simple life of being your little child who had the luxury of you thinking for her, making decisions for her, and scheduling her daily activities. Instead of having to think and make decisions for herself, she just had to follow your orders and do whatever she was told.

You made sure he got up in time, and didn't miss the bus to school. You drove him to his recreational activities and stayed to watch or cheer him on. You also got him home safely afterwards.

Once their bodies begin to change and that alarm clock signals the beginning of adulthood, teenagers begin to reject all the things they relate to their childhood and being a child. They no longer want parents to do things for them, or to be at their sports events. They stop following parents' advice because, in their minds, that would be the same as still being a child and not a growing adult.

Like a string that has been cut and bounces up and down a few times before settling, your teenager's emotions will go up and down constantly, until they have figured out who they are and where they are in life. Your teenager will begin leaving their childhood practices and try to work more on their adult life situations. They are learning to be more independent, and will try to discover and recognize their individual personality.

We parents sometimes think that this is a stage of life

where what we say and do will have no affect. That is not necessarily true. It is more important now than ever to show your teenager love and support. Show your teen that he has a wonderful support system that will always be there for him no matter what.

Your support lessens the chances that she will make a mistake. Even if she does have a lapse in judgment, your support will let her immediately come to you before any part of the situation gets worse.

A teenager who is confident in your support will think situations through more clearly, be less prone to any form of peer pressure, and will therefore get into less trouble than a teenager who feels that he must deal with everything on his own.

Accepting Teenage Behavior

Try not to ask your teen, "What has gotten into you?" or "What were you thinking?" Your teenager is someone who is extremely confused, and is just trying to come out of life still sane. Asking them these questions just reminds them that you do not believe in their decisions or thoughts, which will make them angry because you should know that they are just learning to make decisions. It also will cause them to feel ashamed and increasingly insecure because you are emphasizing that they are not making the right choices.

The only answer your teen is going to give you to questions such as those is "I don't know." Do not be annoyed with this answer because the truth is, your teenager really doesn't know.

Reprimanding them by pointing out that they are not responding to your suggestions in the manner they used to will only prove to them that they are on the correct path to not being a child anymore. In order to successfully guide your teenager through puberty and to teach them how to be a responsible adult, we have to treat our teenagers in a different manner than when they were children.

Remember that your teenager is trying to cast off their childhood ways. It would be a great benefit to your relationship if you can also detach yourself from looking at your son or daughter as a child, and look at them instead as a young person who is starting out on a new life with a blank slate.

When your child was an infant, you either carried him or pushed him in a stroller. You fed him until he was able to take the spoon and feed himself. You changed his diapers until he was toilet-trained. You were at your toddler's side as he went through all these stages of physical development—no pushing, just patiently waiting until he was ready to go to the next step.

Teenage years are the same as the toddler stage—just another natural, physical process of development that every person goes through in their life. But the teens are an age of huge process of mental development. Now your child needs to learn how to compare, choose, decide, act, and react on her own two feet.

Just as when they were learning to walk, and you lent them a hand, now they need to learn how to think independently and desperately need to borrow your head. Since your teenager is truly lost at this point in his life, he will gladly accept a parents' support and help as long as it is offered in a way that is true guidance and is suggested in a supportive way. As soon as your teenager feels pushed back into a childlike role, he will retract and try to get away from you and the pressure you are putting on him.

Your teenager's friends and classmates also play a huge role during this stage of life. Your teen can identify with them since they are going through the same emotional turmoil. Your son or daughter also believes that they must have their friends' approval that they are doing well.

As adults, we have had enough experience to know how to react properly in various situations and how to deal with difficult people. Your teen needs your experience now, and there is a way to guide your teenager without being obvious about it. Similar to making small talk, you should ask questions in a way that will encourage them to respond and think for themselves and will not make them feel as though they are being strung along.

We parents also need to tell our teenagers over and over again that no matter what happens, we will always stand by and support them. They need to know that they can call upon us for help no matter what the situation or time, without the fear of being ridiculed or punished. In no way can we prevent our teenagers from getting themselves into a difficult situation, but we can be there to help them like a good friend.

However, there is no guarantee that they will always come

to you for help. Your teenager's world is expanding, and they are meeting new people who they may feel they can trust. Some of these new sources may have good advice and information, and some may not. It would be unrealistic to believe that your teenager will always be able to tell the difference. They have not yet experienced bad advice since we parents have always been the ones to help them.

Our teenagers do not yet know, or fully comprehend, that there are people who may purposely try to lure them into difficult and unsafe situations. Your young teen is taking baby steps into a world of difficult decisions and they will fall quite a bit. Since we want our teens to come to us, we cannot scold them for these falls. Instead we should praise them for trying and give them the proper advice—while at the same time thank them for putting their trust in our suggestions and us.

When the time comes that your teenager has done something wrong, made a bad decision, or gotten into trouble, try your best not to remark that he should have known better. They really do not know better—they have no experience!

By the time your teen comes to you and the decision has already been made, there is no point in yelling or scolding. Now is the time where you can help her where her judgment lapsed, and give her advice on how to better handle the situation if it arises again. Scolding or punishing her for being honest about a situation will only cause her to lose faith in you—and not return for help the next time.

Imagine yourself having difficulties with a particular task at work. At your next meeting, you mention to your supervisors that you are having trouble with this particular task. One supervisor offers to go over it with you a couple of times to make sure you understand all the steps involved in the process and offers to get you additional help or training if needed. Supervisor #2 scolds you for not knowing the process by now, proclaims he does not have the time to help you with this task, and wonders how you got the position in the first place. Which supervisor would you turn to the next time you are in need of help or advice?

Teaching your child early on that he can come to you for help and advice is like a security blanket for him later on. He will not be afraid to make decisions, and will come to you as soon as he even suspects that he may be in trouble. As your child's trust in you grows, he will be less likely to seek the advice of his friends and to succumb to any of their negative temptations.

In the following chapters, I will illustrate some of the most common trouble areas between parents and their teens. I will examine the reasons why there is a problem to begin with, how your teenager sees the situation, how we parents can overcome the obstacle at hand, and how to resolve the situation and bring it to a win-win ending. You also will find out how to get and keep your teenager coming to you for advice and input in his daily life. You will see how you can make your teenager understand that you truly want the best for him. The following chapters are interactive situations, and the examples are meant to illustrate how parents should interact with teenagers in order to build a successful relationship.

Prepare yourself to be angry and disappointed without showing it to your teen; to hold in what you really want to say about a situation; to take a deep breath and talk with your teenager calmly; to never push him or her into making a decision but just support them with gentle guidance.

I will show you how to lay out the options, explain possible outcomes, and leave the choice up to them—even if to you, the right choice is as clear as day. You will see how to stand back and hold your breath while you wait for a decision, hoping with all your heart that it is the right one. You will learn how to overcome disappointment when your teen makes a mistake, put aside your pain, and gather the energy to lift your teenager up and encourage her through everything that will be coming her way through these difficult years.

CHAPTER II
Connecting With Your Teenager

Communication is the most important element in building a successful relationship with your teenager. The expression, "It is not what you say, but how you say it," has never been more true or more applicable than here. As we talk with our teens, we can either give them a sense of compassion, understanding, and support; or we can convey to them that we are disappointed and angry about what they did, and that they aren't doing what we told them to. The way we respond to, or address, our teenagers will determine if they will come to us for answers and advice the next time.

Your teenager will be the one giving you the cues when he wants your help and when not. He will also make ample use of the three favorite teenage answers. These are "I'm fine", "I don't know" and "Nothing." There is no urgency or a cry for help in these answers. Your teen might not feel like talking, and it is up to the parent if they want to start a conversation or not.

However, there are a couple of phrases your teenager may use that express that he is disappointed, or even insulted, with the way the discussion is going. These two are "Whatever you say" and "You just don't understand."

Both of these answers are a clear statement from your teen that he thinks he has absolutely no input in matters that concern his daily activities. He is telling you that you are treating him like a child and are not giving him a chance to state any of his thoughts on the subject at hand. He also is stating that, in his opinion, you are just not listening to him at all.

Should you hear any of these, you need to take a quick inventory of what was said and ask yourself where you cut your teenager off or out—or didn't listen to or hear his side of the story. These comments are a big STOP sign. If you cannot recall with what exactly you turned your teenager off, ask him. He also will have to overcome being hesitant to talk things out. But as his trust that you are really interested in finding out what goes on in his life and mind grows, it will be easier and easier to get a response.

A common complaint from parents is that their teenager does not talk to them anymore. An advertisement against teenage smoking on TV touched that sentiment with the following statement—"At age four you could not get them to stop talking; at age 16 you cannot get them to talk."

First, the teenager is not sure how to approach us parents with their problems. They do not know how to differentiate between too much dependency—"running to mommy and daddy"—from talking choices and situations over with parents.

Secondly, our own busy lifestyles might have given our children the impression that we do not have enough time to listen to their problems. Thinking back, how many times has your child approached you with a question, news or story, and your response was either, "Not now, honey," or, "I'm busy right now." Perhaps you promised to listen to them as soon as you were finished with what you were doing right then—and did not.

The more often we sent our child away, the more he learned not to bother us with his problems and questions. Now that we want him to come to us, we will have to start repairing the damage. We need to convince our teenager that we indeed care and want to listen to him and will make time for him.

Another important factor that needs to be considered is that our teenager does not think at our level. Most parents of teenagers are around 40 years old. We have had plenty of emotional ups and downs during our lifetime, and have a different perspective about what is important and what we just need to get over.

However, we never forget our first love, and how much it hurt when it ended. We remember, because at that time, our world was so small that our emotions proportionately were a lot more serious.

Your teenager is at that point right now—the smallest thing means the end of the world. We need to transform our thoughts and get to their level of feeling in order to successfully relate and talk to them.

It is true that the problems we have to deal with in our daily lives make our teenagers' problems seem trivial. We have to remind ourselves every day that the problems that our teenager faces are just as important to your teen as the problems we face.

In other words, school and friends are tremendous pressures in your teenager's life, and he does not have the necessary experience to deal with his everyday stress. As adults, we moved onto much bigger problems, but your teenager is dealing with his problems now.

Our quick response when our daughter is trying to tell us about a particular problem she is facing in school is to "not take it serious, you'll laugh about it in 10 years." Your daughter needs a solution now, not in 10 years. She is dealing with an emotional emergency or a situation in school or with her friend now. Since our teenagers do not know how to handle the situation, they come to us for help, advice and, most of all, emotional support.

Parents have to deal with many problems of the adult world. We have the burden of providing for our family. Some of us have very demanding and stressful jobs, and many parents are unhappy with their place of work. When we come home, all we want is peace, quiet and relaxation.

When your teen starts to talk to you as soon as you walk in the door, it is very tempting to ask her to give you a few minutes to settle in and you will have time for them in a little bit. Your child will go away and leave you alone. When you are ready to pick up the conversation and ask "So, now tell me what happened today," you will notice that the enthusiasm about the story is gone. You also will most likely only get half the story, potentially missing some very important information.

A gigantic step towards open, enthusiastic and productive conversations with your teen will be if you stop what you are doing when your teenager approaches you with a story or a question, and pay full and complete attention. They need to feel that they are more important to us than being on the computer, watching TV, or paying bills.

We adults engage in activities in our spare time to distract us from our daily problems, relax us and give us the opportunity to tune out the world. You will be surprised to find that it is very refreshing to listen to your and other teenagers. Take the time to listen to their problems and to see their world through their eyes.

You will come to appreciate what a wonderful, carefree time teenage years are—still living at home, being provided for, yet starting to develop their own personality and to act independently. Your teenager gives you the opportunity to re-live those carefree years. Put the problems of today away and out of your mind and enjoy your teen.

Developing Conversations

If you feel that your teenager does not talk to you or does not come to you with problems that he is facing, you will have to start building the bridge that will connect you and your teen. One very easy way to start a conversation is to ask questions. If you are at a point of not talking to each other at all, your questions will have to be broken down into small segments. You might have to pull the answers out of your teenager in the beginning.

Once your teenager begins to understand that you want to know what goes on in his life and that he cannot shut you out with one-word answers, he will be giving you answers more and more voluntarily. It is your persistence that will get your teenager to talk with you more and more.

Imagine that your teenager just came home from school, or you just came home from work. To your question, "How are you?" the answer is "Fine." You ask, "Anything happen in school today?" the reply is "Nothing." Even if the school happened to burn down that day, you still will get "Nothing."

It is up to you to start the conversation. Ask "Did you not have a test today?" if you are keeping up with her school schedule. Ask her how she feels she did on the test. You can ask what subjects she had. Ask if she has a lot of homework. "How is the teacher?" "What do your friends think about that teacher?" "How many other kids in your class did not pass this test?" "How many other kids in your class had As?" Ask if she needs help studying.

My daughters, for example, wrote flash cards whenever they had to study verbs, and I quizzed them. All I asked of them is to give me a day's notice so I could arrange my day accordingly. This way I did not feel pressured and having to squeeze them into my day, and they learned to respect my time and to plan for certain events. When we sat down at the agreed upon time, both of us were relaxed, and we focused completely on the task at hand.

I cannot think of a better way to show your child that you are interested in their academic success than that you are willing to do what it takes to help them be successful. Once your child realizes that you are genuinely interested and that you are willing to help any way you can, they will open up to you and discuss difficulties with you on an ongoing basis.

Using my daughter again as an example, she was never particularly interested in math, but managed to get average grades. When faced with geometry in 11th grade, we soon realized that she had very little chance of getting a passing grade. Realizing that she truly was not interested in this particular subject, I had several options to respond to her failing grade. Knowing that math was not her strongest side, I had to consider if I really wanted to put myself into the position of fighting a turbulent and loosing battle by insisting that she had to get a good grade in geometry. At that point, she had chosen her field of study for college, and math did not play a major role in that.

I decided to ask her what grade she thought she could reasonably achieve if she had the necessary help. I did tell her that with the necessary help I was referring to a tutor from a nearby college. To my surprise, she told me she thought that she would be able to achieve a "C" or better.

She worked with a tutor with enthusiasm, and finished 11th grade with a "C" in geometry. I succeeded by putting her in charge of her grade. She embraced the challenge and accepted the tutor, eager to prove to me that she could take care of her affairs.

However, you first have to get your teenager to talk. Suppose your daughter has been rather depressed for a couple of days. Her usual smile and sunny disposition are gone. You can tell that something is bothering her. So you approach her with "What's wrong, honey?" and get the usual "Nothing" in return.

Don't stop there, but keep on trying to find out what is bothering her. You can say "Nothing? I can see that you have not been your usual happy self these last days. Something is on your mind that is troubling you, and I really would like to help you." You will probably get something like "No-one can help", or "There is nothing you can do."

Continue to try to get the point across to your teenager that whether or not you can help depends on the situation. You might have some ideas to help. Even if you cannot do anything to change the situation, everyone is helped sometimes just by having someone to listen. Then ask her if there is anything you can do to make her feel better, like making an ice cream sundae, or renting a really sappy movie so you both can cry your eyes out.

Our children want to talk to us and want our help. After all, we are their first point of reference. They know us. They have lived with us for years. Unless it is something really pressing, they will approach us when it appears to them that we have time to listen.

My older daughter preferred to talk to me while I was making dinner. The younger one was most willing to talk to me as soon as I got home, and she still does today. As much as we parents want to relax and unwind from the day at work, we must remind ourselves that if we are not going to listen to our teen when they are ready to talk to us—if we send them away at that moment—we give our children the message that our priorities are more important to us than they are.

Once we parents get accustomed to the idea that we need to be there when our children need us, it will be easier and easier for us to just shut off what we are doing, and give our children 100 percent of our attention. We need to let our teenagers know that they matter, that we take them seriously, and that we are there to help and gladly support them whenever they need it. It will give them the confidence and courage they need, and it will strengthen the bond between you and your child tremendously. You will have a satisfied smile on your face after a successful conversation, when you and your teenager part happily.

All you have to invest in order to achieve this success is time and patience. Since I was, and still am a single mother, we never had any extra money to buy things that other children had. There never was a Nintendo or PlayStation in our house, nor did my children have the latest fashions or gadgets. I firmly believe that no matter how much money we spend on our children to show them that we love them, nothing is more important than investing our time into them. Only when we make them a part of our daily routine and allocate the time they need for them will we earn their respect, love, and trust.

So if your teenager wants to tell you what happened in school, or what so-and-so did, let him talk and really listen. You will learn what and how your child thinks, and you will learn about their peers. You will learn how they are doing in school, what teachers they like, which ones they dislike, what subjects they do well in and where they need help. The more you know about your teenager and his friends, the easier it will be for you to realize potential problems and start discussing the situation with your son or daughter.

Listening To Your Teenager

One day your teenager comes home from school and tells you that one of his friends started to smoke. Your immediate response may be to tell your son that he better not be smoking, and that if you ever catch him you will punish him one way or another.

Your teenager's response in this case is going to be something like: "Sure, dad," and he will turn and walk away. Now you wonder if he is planning to take up smoking and worry about it. Your teenager is frustrated because you treated him like a child by lecturing instead of listening.

These events will lead to a stressed relationship, constant confrontation, and total frustration for you as well as your teenager.

If your teenager approaches you with a story or lets you know about something a friend is doing, you can be assured that they have an opinion about the particular situation. You need to find out what they are thinking and how they see the situation before you agree or disagree with them.

Asking them what they think about it also gives you the time, if necessary, to collect yourself from the surprise of anything your teenager just told you. More importantly, it gives you an opportunity to find out your teenager's values, thoughts, and opinions. You will have a clear understanding of how many of the values that you tried to instill in your child have been adopted. Most important, you give your teen the message that you are interested in his opinion and want to hear it. He will be less hesitant to approach you the next time around, eager to talk about whatever is on his mind, discuss it with you and thus draw on your knowledge.

Consider that your teen may have come to you about the "friend smoking" situation to talk about how disappointed he is in his friend or how angry he is with his friend because he knows that smoking is unhealthy. Your teen may want, or more importantly may need, you to tell him how proud you are of his choice not to smoke.

This may be one of the situations where your teen needs your support and understanding. While you may want to yell at him about how naive his friend is being and how you do not want your teenager hanging out with him, you need to consider the fact that those same thoughts may be in your teen's mind as well. Your teenager has thoughts and opinions about what is going on in his life, and you can only find out by listening.

Once your teenager is comfortable talking with you, you will hear a lot of things that you would rather ignore, that will make your hair stand up in the back of your neck and tempt you to react with parental discipline instead of as a friend and mentor of your teenager. The choice is always yours, and I cannot possibly tell you how to choose. Just be aware that judgment, threats, and punishment will shut down the flow of communication that you worked so hard to build.

Your teenager will hesitate to talk with you about something that is troubling him, because you might punish or judge him before he has the opportunity to tell you what he thinks about it. You will not get the chance to get to know your teenager, or have any idea about his values and beliefs. You will not be able to relax in the knowledge that he has "a good head on his shoulders." You also cut yourself out of the opportunity to share or have any input in your son's or daughter's future.

We parents must realize that we really do not have control anymore over our teen's actions. Your teenager will do whatever he deems right, with or without your input. Your only way to offer guidance to your teenager now is when he is willing to listen to you; but in order to get him to listen to you and your opinion, you have to listen to your teenager and his opinion also.

CHAPTER III
Giving Your Teenager Room To Grow

Throughout my years of employment, all my supervisors had one thing in common. When I approached them with a problem, they wanted me to present one or more possible solutions.

Being able to figure out a way to solve a problem is a very important part of independent living, and I have my father to thank for teaching me this trait. I vividly remember that every time I went to my dad with a problem, he would sit down with me and have me list possible actions and possible outcomes and consequences.

At first I found this very frustrating. After all, I had come to my dad to get a quick answer, a quick fix. I wanted him, with his experience, to think for me. Yet he sat me down and made me think for myself. After a few times of going through that process, I realized it was not that hard. It actually was fun to toss various scenarios around with him and then decide on the option that seemed best.

To keep your teenager's interest and to keep him coming to you with his questions, he needs an active part in each experience. Parents need patience to step back and let the teenager handle the situation—but stay at a safe distance, keeping a watchful eye on him. You want to be able to assist if necessary, but not interfere in his quest to complete a task.

Patience is of utmost importance. Parents might be able to complete a particular task in a few minutes, whereas it will take a teenager hours, maybe days, to figure out a solution. It might be a good idea to consider this before giving a particular task to him. We can ask how the project is coming along. Depending on the task, we might suggest books or the Internet for information. We can ask questions to guide him along or to help him find the answer if necessary, but we must bite our tongue and wait and not decide for him.

Begin With Small Tasks

Girls and boys alike will change their eating habits. Some change them because their friends are while others just want to have some input in what we make for dinner. This is just one of their ways of letting us parents know that they now have an opinion.

I have seen, and still do see, parents standing in the aisle of the supermarket involved in an argument with their teenager. I have found if giving your teenager an active part in the weekly ritual of food shopping greatly cuts down on these scenes.

When deciding on what to make for dinner, let your teenager have some input. For example, if you were planning on making roast beef, ask him what side dishes he would like. If he complains about what snacks you buy or do not buy, tell him to add whatever snacks he wants to the shopping list. If he still complains, you can point out that you got what was on the list. You will not have a bad conscience, and your teen will learn that it is now his responsibility to let you know what he wants.

Another example of a simple task is reprogramming the cell phone. My younger daughter, then 14, switched cellphones, and needed assistance with reprogramming her phone. Instead of taking her phone and calling the provider, I gave her the number and told her to call herself. To ease some of her nervousness I explained the process to her, that she would have to go through several choices on the menu, to have all parts ready, and that she will be asked some security questions. I told her to call me once she got to that point. I would be close enough to hear her calling if she needed me. After she had wiggled her way through the menus she did call me for the answers to the security questions. Once they were answered, I left. A few minutes later, when she walked by me,

I asked her "How did it go?" Proudly she answered, "I am all set."

If we are willing to step back and let our teenager handle certain situations, we also have to be aware that there is a very good chance they will do the task differently than we would. For some parents, it will not be easy at all to let your teenager find his way when you know what works. Try not to tell him he is doing it wrong or that it will not work that way. Either your teenager will prove to you that there is another way to come to the same result, or he will have to admit, after several wasted hours, that your way is the right way after all.

The daughter of one of my friends had helped her in the kitchen since she was eight years old, and had followed her detailed instructions without a question. Around age 13, she started to slice the ingredients for the salad different than her mother had taught her. My friend was very upset that her daughter was slicing ingredients in large pieces, because she thought they tasted awful that way. My friend tried everything, from threats to punishment, to get her daughter to slice the various vegetables the way she wanted. She even said it was her kitchen and she had the final say of what was going to be cooked and how.

It was not easy to listen to the two of them—one insisting that she had years of experience and knew what worked best, the other refusing to just take over her mother's way of cooking without being allowed any kind of individuality. It took some time to get my friend to accept that a dish, prepared by her daughter, was not a direct reflection on her own cooking abilities. My friend had to learn to step aside and share the kitchen with her daughter. As she gave her daughter more and more freedom, it did not take long at all until they decided on menus together. They also picked who would make what dish before starting.

Once my friend did not focus on how it was done anymore, both of them looked forward to cooking together. It was their time to chat uninterrupted and have some "girl time."

By giving your teenager more responsibility and allowing them to handle more and more situations by themselves, their self-esteem and confidence will increase with every successfully completed task. As they get older and physically stronger, we parents can increase the tasks and responsibility according to our teen's abilities.

A friend of mine is a very good auto mechanic and took care of all the repairs on his cars. His son, then 15, had initially shown interested, but lately avoided helping him. When we discussed this a little further, we discovered that my friend had been too quick to interfere when his son tried to fix something on his car. His son, discouraged and doubting his own abilities because of the multiple interruptions, thought that he did not understand enough about cars and he better leave it to his dad or a professional mechanic.

Once my friend realized that his interferences had discouraged rather than taught his son, they talked about it and decided to work on both their cars at the same time. My friend said that this worked out great—since his attention was on his car, he could not look over his son's shoulder. Since they were practically side-by-side, they talked almost all the time. My friend also could not help noticing how handy his son was. He also confirmed that this positive time together carried over into other activities and, before long, they were doing more things together and talked a lot more.

Girls are usually more interested in fashion and makeup. When they were small, they snuck into your bathroom and used your lipstick and blush. Now they have their own makeup and still are experimenting a lot. Magazines give examples of creating your own special look and every magazine has different ideas about it.

One of my friends thought that her daughter was using too much makeup. She had tried to talk to her daughter about it and had been told that she did not understand what was in fashion. When she complained to me about it, I suggested a makeup party, inviting her daughter's friends and their mothers. She reserved the whole afternoon for this party and asked a makeup artist to come by and work with a few of the girls and mothers individually. The party turned out to be a lasting success. My friend's daughter was very happy that her mother had taken so much interest in her and her friends, and her friends envied her for having such an open-minded mom.

If you would rather talk to your daughter yourself about fashion and make-up, here are a few suggestions. Start out with asking what the latest trends in makeup are. To stay informed and make sure you are not using outdated styles, ask your teenager for the newest hairstyles, makeup and fashion trends. Most likely, she will have plenty of magazines that illustrate the newest trends. Look through them with your daughter, and discuss them. Your daughter might have a few ideas how to update your look, and you might have fun trying it out. Since you show interest in her opinion and you are working together on your new looks, your daughter will be much more inclined to listen to your advice than if you just told her to use less makeup.

Some situations will depend on who delivers the message as to whether your teenager listens or not. Since your teenager will assume that you are trying to talk her out of using so much makeup, she might be defensive from the start and not lend an open ear to your suggestions or reasons. In my friend's case having a professional makeup artist make the suggestions ensured they were received with an open mind as positive information.

Another friend of mine is an accomplished rider and her son had been riding for a few years, too. She found that while her son had good control of his horse, he lacked style and posture. Naturally, my friend tried to give him lessons on how to improve. She found that her son was either saying yes to her instructions but not following through, or he would argue with her. I explained to her that, to her son, it felt like she was telling him what to do, that he did not see it as lesson because his parent gave it. She decided to sign him up for riding lessons at a nearby farm. Even though my friend asked the riding instructor to concentrate on the areas her son needed to improve, because the lesson itself was delivered by a third party, her son received it with an open mind.

During some of my meetings with teenagers and their parents, I found that some parents answered the questions I asked their teens. One of them was a very good tennis player and had won some awards. Every time I asked him a question, his father would answer it. After a while the teen left and his father did not understand why.

When I asked him if he was aware that he had answered two of the questions I had directed to his son, he answered, "Of course." He went on to explain, "My son never says more than a word. He never mentions the awards and trophies he has received."

I suggested that his son most likely left because he had not given him the chance to express how he felt about his accomplishments. Since he jumped in to answer instead of giving his son a chance to talk for himself, he had emphasized to his son that he thought he was incapable of answering for himself.

He was now caught in a circle; his son was not speaking because the father spoke for him, and the father answered because the son did not. I suggested that he talk with his son and explain the situation to him. Since his son received many compliments for his accomplishments, maybe they could practice a few responses. This exercise would help his son to overcome his fear of saying something wrong, and would get the father used to waiting for his son's answer. When I met the father a few weeks later, he told me that talking with his son had not only solved this problem, but that his son was opening up to him and asking him for advice in other matters also.

When Parents Try Too Hard

Here are a couple of examples to illustrate how teenagers sometimes will make choices with the sole purpose of forcing their parents to give them more freedom and opportunities to decide for themselves. They rebel against too tight restrictions and try to get their parents to listen to them and allow them some input in their own lives. Unfortunately, they focus only on rebelling. With a tunnel vision, they wait to be heard and trusted by their parents—not seeing the damage they do to their own life and future along the way.

I got to know one of my daughter's friends and her parents since she and my daughter attended ninth grade together. Her friend was the oldest of three children. When I first met her, she was an honor student with straight As.

As her body matured, her father became more and more protective. Completely focused on keeping his daughter safe, unfortunately he discounted her abilities, good sense and judgment. He tried to protect her by setting rules of where she could go and when. He was extremely strict about her being home on time, not hesitating to embarrass her by calling the parents of her friends if she was not home at the time he set.

Needless to say, father and daughter had many arguments. Her mother supported her and also tried to reason with her husband, but she was not able to get him to allow their daughter some freedom in her choices. During 11th grade her grades began to drop, and by the 12th grade it was questionable if she was going to be able to graduate. Fortunately she did graduate.

When I spoke with her mother the following summer, she said that she wanted so badly for her daughter to go to college. She wanted a better life for her daughter than her own, having babies at an early age with a minimal education.

My daughter's friend planned on going to the local

community college and becoming a registered nurse in obstetrics, and work at the nearby hospital. Instead, she moved in with her boyfriend of only five months as soon as she was 18, and became engaged.

My daughter told me her friend had only moved out of her parent's house to get out from her father's control. She became pregnant and had her first child at 19. She and her fiancée both work minimum wage jobs to support themselves and their newborn baby, and live in a one bedroom apartment.

The father wanted to steer his daughter in the right direction, but used force instead of guidance to do so. By just setting rules and demanding that they be obeyed, he drove his daughter out of the house and out into a life that none of them—father, mother or daughter—wanted for her.

The father of another friend tried to isolate his daughter. She was not permitted to go over to any of her friend's houses or have her friends come to her house unless her father or mother were present or with her the entire time. Given that both her parents worked, she did not have much contact with her friends outside of school, so she made the most of every opportunity she had. After she turned 15, her father started to watch every move she made. Whenever possible, he would take his daughter with him and watch her and how she interacted with people. She told me that it felt to her like a lion in wait, ready to pounce should she make a wrong move. When her father talked with her most of his phrases and questions ended with "Didn't you?" or "Don't you."

In his mistrust towards her he went so far as to watching her with his binoculars while she was walking the beach where the entire family spent their vacations. He thought his daughter did not know, but she had seen him looking in her direction with them on several occasions. She had not dared to ask her father why he was doing that and he never mentioned it to her. She was mad and hurt that he was going that far.

The summer when she was 17, she was strolling along the

beach and ran into the group of young teenage boys that were playing in the band at her hotel. Since she was a pretty girl, they had noticed her and she found one of them especially cute. So she sat down with them and talked with them for quite a while. The next day when she met them at the beach again, they told her that her father had approached them and threatened them if they would not stay away from her. She was outraged that her father would not allow her any freedom at all. To get back at him she asked the boys to take a walk with her and to be careful to stay out of her father's vision. She too moved out of her parent's house on her 18th birthday.

I had several discussions with fathers about their teenage daughters and why they are so overprotective of them. I came to understand that fathers do not fear what their daughter might do, but what boys will do to their daughters. In other words, fathers know what goes on in a boy's mind and that makes them afraid for their daughters.

As much as I can understand their concern, it is up to the father to explain this to his daughter. It is not necessary to paint an ugly picture, but girls need to know that the way they dress does affect how boys perceive them. Girls need the male perspective to understand that being popular should not be confused with how many boys they have sex with. Tell them how boys really feel about girls that are willing to have sex.

If you are a single mom, ask within your circle of male friends. The message is more powerful and believable if it comes from a man.

By setting rules and expecting them to be obeyed or not allowing your daughter any contact with other teenagers at all, your daughter will focus on breaking out from under your control. On the other hand, if a daughter understands her father's concern, she will appreciate his protection, and make sure that he knows where she is and what she is doing most of the time.

She will also be more aware of the opposite gender and be careful not to provoke them by dressing provocatively or teasing them in any other way.

It is just as important for moms to share with sons how girls think. A comment from your son that he just does not understand girls or that they are so weird is a perfect opportunity to start a conversation. Ask him why he is making that remark, and listen to his answer. Soon you will be transformed back into a young girl yourself, remembering all the shy glances and messages you exchanged with your friends when you were in high school.

CHAPTER IV
Your Teenager's Friends

As your teenager develops his personality, he will oppose taking part in family activities, preferring to spend time with friends. This is not because he suddenly does not like you anymore. At this point in his life, he feels that he can relate better to friends who are close to his age. Plus his friends will make fun of him if he spends too much time with his parents. Your teenager's insecurity makes him very vulnerable to his friends' opinions, since he measures his individuality by how well his friends accept him, and how popular he is.

As mature adults, we had many years of experience dealing with friends, relatives and co-workers. We encountered different personalities and learned how to interact with them. We saw people succeed and we saw some fail. We learned by experience which actions bring us to success, and which lead to failure.

As we look at our teenager, we want so badly to pass these experiences on to our child. Our parental instinct wants to prevent her from making the wrong decisions or saying the wrong thing. We want to save her from bad experiences and harm.

Since we cannot be hooked up to a machine for an instant experience transfer, we have to do it the old fashioned way. We need to talk with our teenager and deal with every situation individually. Every day gives us opportunity to teach them a little bit more and parents need to take full advantage of it. Utilize the three elements that you have established with your teenager up to this point: good communication between you and your teen, a relationship that tolerates and respects each other's opinions and the social values that you instilled in your teenager.

Staying informed about what is going on in your teenager's life is absolutely necessary. Only by talking with your son or daughter about various situations and about their friends will give you the opportunity to guide them. Keep asking questions about their friends. Invite their friends over so you can get a first-hand feel for them. Talk with their friends and meet their friends' parents if you get the opportunity. You will make some new friends for yourself that way, too.

Having a barbecue is a perfect opportunity and setting for your teenager to have some of his friends and their families over for a nice day of good food and conversation. Besides meeting the parents, you also get to know some of your teen's friends in a casual setting.

Some of my daughter's friends were shy and quiet, others blended with every crowd and then she had a couple of friends who were the entertainers. These two kept making fun of everything, including my daughter's habits.

As entertaining as this was for me, I had to be very careful not to chime in with them. I could laugh about their jokes, but I could not tell them that they were right, because that would have hurt my daughter's feelings very much. I would have sided with her friends instead of being in "her corner."

Imagine how hard it is for adults to laugh with someone who just made a joke about us. A person must be very confident to be able to do so. Your teenager, whose confidence level is very low, would be devastated if you make fun of her in front of her friends.

As you get to know your teens' friends more and more, it will bring your son or daughter much closer to you, because you are interacting with and accepting their friends. The second advantage is that it will give you another opportunity to keep the communication going with your teenager.

Now you can ask how their friends are doing. Since you now know them, you also can ask personal questions. You will get the chance to discuss their friends' choices with your teen. That gives you the opportunity to talk about various subjects and listen to your teen's opinion, and explain your opinion and the experiences it is based on.

Most likely you will not agree with all their choices of friends. Your son or daughter might be spending time with some kids who you fear will be a bad influence. We recognize if a particular kid is "heading for trouble" because our years of experience have taught us consequences of actions from various people. Our teenager, however, does not have this experience.

A statement from you that a particular friend is "no good" will only get you a blank stare in return. This isn't due to rebellion or anger, but because your teen really does not know the definition of "no good".

If we try to take a shortcut and simply forbid them to hang out with this particular kid, we will drive them away from us. We give them the impression that we do not think that they are capable of choosing their friends. It also will create a hostile environment. By confronting our teens, we are putting them in an either/or situation. We force them to choose between obeying us and sticking by their friend.

No matter which way they decide, their decision will not make them happy. They will feel pushed back into the little child role if they obey us and will resent us for it. If they choose to ignore our parental input, they will take the side of that friend and spend even more time with him. Our teenager might realize sooner or later what we meant by "no good", but by that time he will most likely already have gotten into trouble.

Your teenager also needs to understand that what friends they choose will impact their lives and their future. They need to understand that all their actions from now on will impact their future as well. Take every opportunity to point out to your son or daughter how important it is for their future to protect themselves from getting into trouble, whether with the law or with teachers. Do not hesitate to spell it out for them. Bring the chain of events before their eyes, so they can see the whole picture and how situations evolve.

Remember they lack your experience. Give them examples, such as a person who is addicted to drugs. Did they loose their job? What kind of job are they able to do? Can or did they go to college? Did they go to rehabilitation? Were they arrested and sent to prison? If so, now they have a criminal record, how are their chances of finding work now? Talk that scenario through with your child, so they can see the possible consequences of trying to fit in by doing drugs.

Repeat as often as you can that your son or daughter needs to keep focused on building their future. He needs to understand that his teachers or you are not affected by whether he has good grades or not, but that it will affect his own future. He needs to know his grades will determine if he will be able to go to college.

Don't be too quick to decide what characters you consider to be correct when it comes to your child's friends. Just as with adults, teens are not always what they appear to be.

My younger daughter had a lot of different types of friends. She hung out with everyone, from the rich preppy kids to the punk-looking skaters. By looking at these two different groups of teens, you might be quick to judge that the ones with the death metal t-shirts, piercings, and skateboards are the wrong choice for your child. You might try to push them to hang out with the high-classed teenagers who wear the expensive top-label clothing and drive brand new cars, or the ones who are the football players and cheerleaders and whom all the teachers think are "just precious."

Over time and from conversations with my daughter, I came to learn that the group I would have favored did not come with a guarantee of character. Some of the "precious," clean-cut friends were the ones involved with alcohol and drugs, whereas the skateboarders rarely, if ever, did anything against the law. Most, if not all, of them were not into the drug scene, but instead were completely against it, calling themselves "straight edge" and things of that sort. I quickly learned that the term straight edge meant they were against things such as smoking and drugs.

If I chose to make my child hang out with the people I thought were correct, my daughter may have been tempted or forced into acts she didn't want to be involved in. Instead, I trusted that she would make the correct choice of friends and she did. She chose the crowd that, although enjoying going to parties and having fun, also enjoyed staying sober and clean.

I knew most of my older daughter's friends and made it a priority to know all the kids my younger daughter was hanging out with. The fact that I kept mixing two of my younger daughter's friends up was amusing for my daughter as well as her friends. As much as I tried, I could not get them straight.

I took this opportunity to let the girls know that I am proof that nobody is perfect. We all make mistakes, no matter how hard we try, how much information we gather, and how much we weigh our options. I also stressed how important it is to get as much information as possible before making a decision.

To this day I refuse to give my daughters a quick answer when they ask my opinion on something. I still ask them a lot of questions about it. It's not that I can't make up my mind, but I want them to think about the subject matter and weigh their options before making a decision. Ultimately they will be following their own mind, not doing what I say.

When they were young, our children followed our instructions blindly. As teenagers, they are trying to think and decide for themselves. They have to combine what little experience they have with information from outside sources and their feelings, and make decisions that could potentially influence the rest of their lives.

If you find that your daughter is too young to decide, ask her opinion. Ask what she thinks she should be allowed, and why she thinks so. Discuss with her what your pros and cons are when suggesting a solution.

Your son or daughter will make decisions on a daily basis. It would be unreasonable to expect them to come to you with every question. As they take risks by deciding, the consequences of a wrong decision can sometimes be prevented if they are still within your range of protection.

In that second when your teenager needs to decide whether or not to steal that car in order to be considered cool by his friends, he must have the necessary knowledge to see the impact this particular action may have on his future. You will not be there to tell him what to do. Your teenager will make that choice.

So stay informed about your teenager's daily activities and friends. You can always start a conversation by asking questions. Listen to his answers. If you're not sure, clarify by asking more questions and always ask his opinion first. Your teen needs to know that you are treating him as a person, that you are not patronizing him, nor consider him incapable of forming an opinion.

Parents need to know how their teens feel about a particular situation. Imagine how comforting it will be to you when you realize that your teenager just assessed a potentially dangerous situation correctly, and that he is capable of making the right choice.

Point out every time how happy you are for them that they made the right choice. Let them know how happy you are that they are focused on building a good future for themselves.

During my daughter's high-school years I kept asking her about her friends. Especially those I had not seen in a while. Sometimes they just had conflicting schedules, but there are a few that my daughter did stop being friends with because they had started to use drugs, or they had gotten into trouble one way or another. As sad as it was to see these young people head down the wrong path in life, I could not help but to be very grateful that my daughter was capable of recognizing they had made the wrong choice.

Until your son or daughter is able to make the right decisions, go over the chain of events with them. Do it patiently, without ridiculing them, patronizing them, or saying "You should have known." Obviously, they did not. No one puts himself or herself in harms way on purpose.

My older daughter once asked me—after I said to her in anger; "You should have known"—"And how exactly should I have known? Where should I have seen it coming?" Once they come to you, they have already realized that they lack the necessary knowledge to make the right choice, or they are already in trouble. It will only drive your child away from you if you start blaming them.

Remember that you are engaged in the ongoing process of teaching your child to become an adult. Keep helping them along the way. When you see a weak or uncompleted issue with your child, pick up on it and help them to overcome that obstacle. You are their teacher and their friend—hopefully, their best friend.

Freedom—I Have a Driver's License

Around age 16, your child and her friends are getting their driving permits and driver's licenses. Now they can go places by themselves, you will not have to drive them anymore. As great as it might sound initially of not having to chauffer them around, the drawback is that you will not know where they are going, or worse, with whom they are going. As long as you had to drive them wherever they needed or wanted to go, you had the advantage of meeting their friends, their parents, and, most likely, waited until it was time to go back home. As inconvenient as this was for you, it did give you the security of knowing where they were and with whom.

After turning 16, their newfound confidence and their lack of experience makes them extremely vulnerable to bad choices and car accidents. As more and more of their friends drive, your son will need to distinguish between the safe driver and the unsafe driver. When adults get in the car with someone, we know if we feel safe with them driving or not, because of our years of driving experience. In order for your teen to make a distinction like that, he needs to have driving experience himself. Have him get a learner's permit as soon as he can, and then let him drive whenever you need to go somewhere, giving him the opportunity to gain driving experience.

When my daughter got her learner's permit, we started out by just making a circle around our block. Three right turns and back home. Once she was comfortable in staying within her lane, we ventured out to the food store, or the mall. As she got more and more accustomed to keeping the car on the road, I gradually exposed her to new driving experiences. Eventually she drove on the Blue Ridge Highway and other mountain roads.

She drove close to 3,000 miles with her learner's permit before she received her driver's license. This is notable not just for the amount of miles she drove, but more so since I had to push her to get her learner's permit. I insisted that she needed to learn how to drive a car and how to safely maneuver through today's traffic. Having that first-hand experience, she would be able to tell the difference between a safe and non-safe driver.

Around my daughter's 17th birthday she told me that she was thinking of going to Daytona Beach, Florida, with some of her friends for the weekend. We lived in Ocala, Florida, at that time and the trip to Daytona is on Route 40. This road has a reputation of many deadly accidents, especially with inexperienced drivers like teenagers.

My daughter had been driving the distance between Ocala and Daytona Beach multiple times, as driver as well as passenger, and was familiar with the dangers of this trip. The hair on my neck stood up straight and I felt a pit in my stomach as soon as I heard my daughter's plan.

In order to gain time and figure out how to approach this situation, I resorted to ask questions. "Who would be driving?" "How did she feel about the driving style of the drivers?" "How many kids per car?" and "How many cars are going to take this trip?" I also reminded her that the danger of being careless increases if a few cars are taking this trip together.

In my mind a war was raging. If I asked her not to go, she would most definitely focus on convincing me to letting her go, loosing sight of the really important issue, which was the danger of that particular road. If, on the other hand, I just told her to go and something were to happen to her, I would never forgive myself.

In the end, I asked her to take the danger of this trip into account and weigh it against the good time she and her friends hoped to have in Daytona Beach when deciding. When I asked a few days later about the trip, she said that she had decided not to go; the risk was not worth it.

She had enough information to make this decision on her own. Knowing the danger of this trip, she valued her safety and future more important than a fun weekend on the beach. While I was quite surprised that she had decided not to go, her decision reinforced my trust in her ability to look out for herself and her safety.

With every day your teenager's world is expanding. He or she is facing opportunities and new situations on a daily basis. Drugs and cars are readily available and the wrong choice can be the difference between a bright future and no future, life or death.

To be able to make the right choice, your teenager must have information. He will seek this information and advice from any source available. Your teen can get this information either from his, themselves immature, friends and stumble from one negative encounter to another; or your teen can come to you for information and guidance. Once your teenager realizes that you care about him and his future he will come to you for guidance, his value to himself will increase and he will think twice before making any ill-advised decisions and taking bad actions.

CHAPTER V
Setting Limits

Most of this book is describing what we parents have to do and how we have to act and react in order to be supportive to our teen. There is another side to growing up. Your teenager needs to learn to fit into society, adapting and obeying laws and rules. Your teenager needs to learn how to respect others and to be considerate of the people around her.

The standards you would like your teenager to live up to is completely your choice. I will not even attempt to make any suggestions in that matter. All I will convey to you in the following pages is how to get your teenagers cooperation in accepting the limits you set and how to come up with rules and guidelines together.

I grew up in Europe and therefore might have been more conservative than the average American parent. Much to both my daughters' dismay, I would not allow them tattoos, body piercings, or uncommonly colored hair. I was also very strict with their clothing. I insisted that they kept in contact with me. They had to call me as soon as they got home from school to let me know they are home safe, or let me know if they spent time at their friends house and give me a contact phone number before the days of cell phones.

We parents have to put ourselves into the right mindset and find the level on which we will be able to relate to our teenager the best. Teenagers have no experience in time management and independent living. We cannot expect our teenagers to know how long they can stay out, and when they have to be asleep in order to be able to get up for school in the morning. Teenagers will just "go with the flow" and do what their friends are doing only because their friends are the group they best relate to at the moment. Therefore, your teen will want to mimic their friends' every move and decision, whether dealing with time, school, or rules and regulations.

Knowing that teenagers are searching for standards to go by, parents have the opportunity to further strengthen the relationship with their teens by working with them in an understanding and suggestive manner. Since every parent's ideals and principals are different, we all have varying limits on what we will and will not allow.

Throughout the years I have spoken with many parents about this subject. Most of them were frustrated because they had allowed their teenager to do whatever they wanted to do until they themselves were at a point where they just could not take it anymore. They had watched their teenagers participate in reckless behavior and poor time management, and only now tried to put a stop to skipping classes, declining grades and staying out until the early morning hours.

All those parents had one thing in common: they did not know where and how to start. Having a teenager in the house does not mean that you have to tolerate everything your teenager does just to keep peace in the house. On the contrary, it is a great benefit to your teenager if you are able to teach him responsibility towards himself and others early on. It is also another opportunity for parents to show our children that we truly care about them and only have their best interests in mind.

Some of the parents I spoke with tried to manipulate their teens by promising to buy them things they wanted. Others forced their kids to obey to their rules by locking them out of the house, taking away privileges, or punishing them. This creates resentment and frustration for your teenager, and will not solve the problem of your teenager's misbehavior. Instead, this act may only cause more angst between you and your teen, leading to fights, arguments and more seriously, a run-away teenager.

Before I start to discuss options on how to work with your teenager on solving these issues, I need to touch on another subject that came up repeatedly in my conversations with parents. Some parents have the tendency to make threats of punishment if their teen disobeys, but then give in too easily at the first test of the limits they had set.

A rule is not looked upon as a limit by a teenager, but as a challenge that is meant to be pushed as far as it can go. With this in mind, be sure you and your child's pride do not clash in these situations, for it only means disaster.

A friend of mine and his son got into an argument about him not being home on time. While arguing my friend threatened his son with, "As long as you live under my roof you will abide by my rules!" With this being said, his son stormed out the door and yelled, "Well go ahead and lock me out then!" "Fine!" yelled my friend and slammed the door shut, locking it. Both father and son stood on both sides of the door, truly believing that within the next few minutes the other is going to break down, apologize, and claim that they were wrong. Instead, after a few minutes his son took off and stayed at a friend's house.

However, I urge all parents to carefully consider if you are really going to follow through on your threat. Your teenager will only respect and take you serious if you follow through with the consequences. Issuing empty threats conveys the message to them that you are just talking and that there is no need to take you seriously, because you never follow through with what you claim anyway.

The biggest obstacle to overcome in successfully setting limits is to find the fine line between what is acceptable to you and still gives your teenager enough freedom. If we box them in with too many rules, they will feel confined and restricted. They will resent us for it and only focus on breaking free.

Curfew

As your teen gains independence "When do I have to be home?" will have to be addressed. Most of the time this is a rhetorical question from your teenager, for they really are not planning on being home when you say. They see this as an opportunity to show you that they really do not have to listen to you anymore and also to see how much freedom you are willing to give them.

A good way to answer this question is: "When do you have to get up tomorrow?" This brings your teen's focus from being out and having fun to getting up for school in the morning.

Another scenario is to ask: "When do you think you'll be home?" Now your teenager has to come up with a time. Let's assume your teenager answers a time that you think is way too late. Instead of cutting him off with a short "That's too late", state your concerns why you think this is too late, and see how your teen responds to it. Eventually you will come up with a time that you both can live with, and your teen is more likely to actually be home by the agreed upon time.

There will be times when your teenager calls you to see if he can stay out beyond the agreed upon time. I have two different suggestions to handle that call, depending on if it is a school night or not. On a school night, I would remind him that you agreed on that time, and that you expect your teen to stick by his promise. This will teach your teen to be more careful when promising something the next time. He also will make sure he knows what he and his friends are planning to do and how long that will take before giving you a time to be home. Should your teen start to argue and possibly whine, you can shorten the time to be out by 15 minutes.

There were a few times when my younger daughter called to be out late longer on school nights. After I said "No" she started to beg and argue. I told her that now she had to be home by 10:15, and if she wanted to argue further we could also make it 10:00. This worked really well, especially since I was the one picking her up from her friend's house. She learned rather quickly to better consider her time and not to argue about it.

My second suggestion is for Friday or Saturday night. Ask your teen why he sees the need to stay out longer. Ask what are they going to do and where are they going to be. Your teen is waiting for a positive answer from you and will be ready to answer your questions. If you decide that it will do no harm if he stays out longer, agree to it. You only have to grant 30 minutes, it does not have to be hours. To your teen these 30 minutes will represent his victory and his being part in the decision.

By the time your teenager and his friends drive themselves, he will have gotten used to being home early during school nights. By that time my daughter's curfew was only a suggested time, with her being able to stay out a bit longer if she called me to let me know.

My younger daughter frequently came home earlier than her suggested curfew. When I commented, "You are home already?" she responded with "I'm tired," or that she had a test tomorrow, or that there was nothing interesting going on and she would rather relax at home. There also were several evenings when she did not go out at all. This gave me an opportunity to let her know that I liked having her around. We could catch up on the events of the week, set plans for the weekend, talk about her and her friends' progress in school, or we would play cards, a board-game, or rent a movie.

Both of my daughter's freedom of determining how long to stay out at night was in direct relation to their performance in school. If they received a C or below on a test, I would ask them the reasons for that mark. If it turned out that they simply did not have enough time to study, their time to spend with friends was reduced and I paid more attention to how much time they spent studying. If they were tired during school and needed more sleep, then we also needed to adjust their curfew.

Your son or daughter will want to know why you are so concerned with their performance in school and will defend themselves by stating that they do not need to be straight "A" students. This gives you the opportunity to remind your teen that his grades are important because colleges look at the entire high school grade average. Starting with 9th grade, he needs to realize that he is working on building his future and setting the conditions that will get him into the college of his choice.

Guide him through the following example. Let him look at the employment advertisements in your local paper. If he would rather search on the computer, there are several different job lists on the Internet. What are the job categories? Let him research the income range for some professions. What level of education is required for certain employment opportunities? Then have him look at employment opportunities that do not require college. What is the salary range for those jobs?

Then ask him to look at apartments and monthly rent rates. Have him add other expenses such as utilities, food, fuel and entertainment. Now have him compare his monthly expenses to either monthly income. He will soon realize that a college education will afford him a much better lifestyle than the income from a non-college job.

If you give your teen a curfew and he has to be home by that time no matter what, he will focus on ways to breaking your rule and staying out later. On the other hand, if your teen has an active part in determining how long he can stay out, he learns time management. Since he has to give you a time to be home, he needs to know what he and his friends are planning to do and how long it will take.

You also teach him to be considerate of other people if you ask him to be quiet when coming home late at night. There should be no loud talking in the driveway, no loud car stereo playing and no slamming of the doors in order not to disturb the sleep of you or your neighbors.

A Teenagers' Room

There are no magic words or actions that will make your teenager's room a neat room. Take comfort in knowing that every single teenager's room is a complete mess by parental standards. To the teenager, the "mess" is just having everything handy. A teenager would loose sight on what they have to wear if clothes were stored away neatly in drawers. Clothes spread out all over the floor allows them to pick an outfit. If I forced my daughters to clean and organize their room, they would do so, but then quickly realize they could never find anything.

I remember once walking into my younger daughter's room at one of its most disastrous moments. I decided this would be a good time to prove to her my point on how messiness gets you nowhere. I began asking her to find things for me, whether it was a specific t-shirt or pair of pants. To my surprise and dismay she found everything I asked of her in record time. My point is that although to us it may seem like their room is a disaster, to the teenager it is organized in their own way.

Some parents I spoke with have tried and failed in keeping their teenager's room neat. A few mothers chose to clean it up at least once a week, only to have it returned to the usual stage of disorder within a couple of days. Other parents would insist that the door be kept shut and would not go in there at all, pretending that their teenager's room did not even exist.

However you decide on handling the cleanliness of your teenager's room, you can still set limits on what they can or cannot do in that room. Should they keep open soda cans, dirty plates, or half-eaten containers of cookies or crackers in their room, you can tell them that this attracts bugs and is unsanitary and ask them to discontinue eating or drinking in their room.

The same goes for playing their stereo. I had plenty of parents that complained that their teenagers would be blasting their stereos and it would drive them crazy. Considering that it is her room, she should be able to play the stereo, but you can agree on a level of loudness that you can tolerate and still is loud enough for your teenager to feel that she gets to listen to her music the way she wants.

I know that it can sometimes be very hard to listen to what the teenagers of today are listening too. My older daughter's choice in music was tolerable, but my younger one has a deep passion for the punk/rock/scream scene of music. The sound of improperly-tuned electric guitars, and nasal-like screaming sometimes made me want to pull my hair out, and I asked her to keep her door closed when listening to her stereo.

Because I did not criticize her choice of music, I found her talking to me about the bands she listened to—whether it was on how much she enjoyed them, a concert they were having that she planned on or wanted to go to, or about the history of the band itself. Sharing her thoughts and opinions about her music with me gave us something to talk about and even bond over.

CHAPTER VI
Enjoying Your Teenager

Teenagers have the reputation of coming up with crazy ideas and thinking unrealistically. Parents also sometimes are tempted not to give them any credibility because of their limited experience with life. We seem to forget that they have lived with us their whole life and have seen our choices and decision-making processes. I specifically remember two times that my daughters clearly expressed an opposing opinion to my action and time proved them right.

It is true that teenagers believe there is a simple solution for everything, but this can be very refreshing since it expresses their uncomplicated, positive way of thinking, still untainted by negative or disappointing experiences. While we parents are set in our ways and have been doing whatever we are doing the same way for years, our teenagers will be able to introduce a refreshing change to our routines if we allow them to.

During the years, one thing was confirmed to me over and over again. Parents who let their teenagers try to solve problems and listened to them and their opinions before making decisions that affected their teenager's lives had a very close relationship with their teenagers. These teens came to their parents first instead of trying to fix a situation and hoping for the best. They also could not wait to discuss what was on their minds with their parents, and listened to their parents' suggestions and reasons far more than teens who were just told what to do. These teens did far better in school and rarely got into trouble.

The advantage for the parents was that they knew exactly what went on in their teen's life. They knew what their teenager was capable of doing and deciding for himself, and where and what he still needed to learn. Their relationship with their teenager was virtually free of conflicts and they spent a lot of time with their teenagers either doing a project together or participating in a particular sport together. It was obvious that these parents and their teens were a team, sticking up for each other whenever a situation called for it. Since these parents were willing to listen to their teens and their ideas, they also were fortunate to having a good time themselves.

Here are a few of these anecdotes I would like to share with you.

After remodeling our house, my daughters got to choose what color they wanted their room painted from a handful of color samples. My older daughter decided on a pale blue, the younger one on green. When my older daughter came home from school one day, she came into her room to see how far along I was with the painting process. After standing there watching me for a few moments, she came over, dipped her hand into the paint-tray, and slapped it onto the wall. "There" she said pointing at her handprint, "Don't say I didn't help you paint."

I looked back and forth between her and the handprint still in a minor state of shock. My first instinct was to yell at her for ruining the job that I had been doing, but after a couple minutes I had to admit that the handprint on the wall actually looked really good. I asked her what she thought of finishing with the pale blue, and then getting a matching, darker blue and 'stenciling' the wall with her handprints.

My younger daughter used dark green for her handprints. It was a unique idea, and it ended up looking very nice. It made their rooms very personal, and I couldn't help but smile when I entered their respective rooms and looked at those handprints.

I was glad that I had carefully considered how to react to my daughter's idea of "helping." If I had yelled at her about ruining the wall, or about being irresponsible and messing up my hard work, we would have missed out on making our house a real "home," filled with unique designs created by us not as the owners, but by us as the family.

***

Every farm needs a tractor, so when we had our horse farm we had to buy one. We ended up buying a riding lawnmower, which was delivered in a huge box crate that looked impossible to open and proved to be quite a challenge. After we were finally able to break into the crate and remove all the packaging, my younger daughter and I found ourselves staring at a completely unassembled lawnmower.

I began to dig for the instructions so that I could start reading them and organize the multitude of pieces to this machine. Since I need glasses only to read, I was constantly removing my glasses to locate the pieces, and putting them back on to read the instructions.

When I started to get really annoyed and voiced my frustration, my daughter took the instruction booklet from my hands and began to read the directions while describing the pieces needed. After a few minutes, she suggested we move the parts and tractor to the shed so I would not have to keep running back and forth to get tools. We moved everything into to the shed and began to assemble what looked like an impossible task. Surprisingly, the assembling of our new lawnmower actually went smooth. My daughter helped install the seat while I mounted the blades into the cutting unit. It was not an easy task, but working together, we managed to completely assemble a riding lawnmower.

Our choosing to work together ended up making a difficult and annoying task pleasurable and fun. Together we were able to joke about the potential mistakes and how it would probably fall apart out in the middle of one of our fields. My daughter enjoyed calling it "her" tractor and rode around on it quite a bit. I even managed to talk her into cutting the lawn a few times.

***

Since we were living on a farm at the time, money was not readily available to buy everything we wanted. Feeding and managing the horses became not only an extremely physical task, but an expensive one also. Surprisingly, my younger daughter accepted the fact that we could not always afford to buy the latest and most expensive trends in clothing. She understood that although she could go to the mall anytime she desired, her ability to buy clothes was not the same. There were times she even suggested ways we could cut down on our spending and I was surprised to find she knew the different prices a store was charging for certain items. In a time where most teenagers would probably throw fits of how "unfair" their life was, I found my daughter accepting and understanding that sometimes-difficult times came around where sacrifices needed to be made.

***

A friend of mine has a 15-year-old son. Even though he and his wife have been divorced for several years, he is a father who is determined to stay in his son's life. He chose to stay in the same town as his former wife and their son and also to stay involved in his son's activities.

One particular activity his son enjoys is building and launching rockets. Both of them found themselves moving on to larger and more experienced models, and were even making formulas to mix their own fuel. To assemble and fly these more advanced rockets requires a few licenses. Since his son was too young, my friend did all the studying and testing in order to get all the proper licenses.

When I asked my friend how he felt about having to study for the licenses, he said that he actually enjoyed it. It gave him something to talk about and teach his son and, as he said with a wink, "I get to be a teenager all over again myself".

Although it may seem like all they must talk about is rockets, he told me how his son was beginning to open up to him about more personal things, like school and his friends, even his girlfriend.

***

Another friend of mine also owns horses. When he became seriously ill, his oldest daughter had to take over the feeding and management of his three horses at 15 years old.

Like most horse owners, he usually caught the horses in the paddock and led them to their stall via halter and lead rope. This process, however, did not work for his daughter. Since the horses were not very familiar with her, they were not too eager to listen to her calls, or stand still so that she may properly apply the halter. She found herself chasing three horses up and down a paddock every time they needed to be brought in for feeding, which for her was very annoying. She put up with the ridiculous charade for a couple of days before approaching her father and telling him about her problem. He said the horses would grow used to her in a few days and she just needed to be patient; however, she decided to find a way to get these horses to come to her.

The next day, when the horses' feeding time came around, she walked to the gate of the paddock with halter in hand. She raised her hands above her head and broke the carrot stick she was holding in half. The horses heard this and began to slowly approach her. Again, she broke the carrot into smaller sections until the horses were finally standing before her.

She carefully placed the proper halter onto the horse and led them into their stalls, giving them each a small piece of carrot as a reward. After a couple more days, the daughter found herself not even needing the carrot anymore. Once the horses saw her they immediately came running over, ready to be brought to their proper home.

***

Summers in Florida are very hot and humid, so when my daughter suggested taking her and some of her friends to float down the river on a tire tube I agreed. Listening to the stories the girls were sharing on the way there I found out that this river is also habitat to snakes and alligators. I asked the girls if they were not afraid to take this ride but was told that none of the animals was aggressive towards people.

Once we reached our destination, I told the girls I would wait for them at the end because I was not too fond of the idea of sharing the river with snakes and alligators. Giving in to the girls protest, I also got a tube and started the float with them. As the girls had predicted, the alligators were only lying on the banks sunning themselves and we only saw one snake hurrying through the water. While floating on the river we saw many turtles huddled on branches in the water and got close to other wildlife. We also stopped a few times to cool off with a short swim, were splashing each other, or tried to form a chain by hanging on to each others tubes. This day turned out to be relaxing and a lot of fun. I got the chance to forget about daily life and its problems and just enjoy the scenery, the girls, the cool water, and myself.

***

Girls like to go shopping, so a trip to the mall on a rainy day is nothing uncommon. One day my older daughter suggested that we go into various stores and try on outfits that we usually would not choose or wear. We spent several hours trying on different clothes and were getting increasingly daring in our choices. If I tried on a skirt, my daughter would come running with a top that I had to try with it and vice versa.

The day turned out to be a lot of laughs with my daughter including the time we took to have lunch. Had I followed my first instinct that this is going to be a waste of time, I would not have had the opportunity to find out about my daughter's taste in clothes in such detail. I also learned which tops and bottoms she found too revealing, easing my mind how she was going to dress once she was shopping on her own.

***

My teenagers, and the many other teenagers I had the pleasure of knowing over the past years, have taught me a few things, too. I learned that everything does not have to be in its perfect place and that dust does wait for a rainy day. It is OK to drop everything, grab the dog and anyone who wants to come along to go for a walk or drive to the beach on a beautiful summer day. I've learned that fun can be found in the strangest and most unexpected situations and that you will not loose your teen's respect if you act silly sometimes—but you will build a lasting friendship.

My older daughter's favorite phrase towards me changed over the years from "Loosen up, Ma" to "Who are you and what have you done to my mother?" Both of my girls have turned out well. They are both warm, caring, straightforward people and my older daughter now is a loving yet strict mother to my grandson.

By reading this book you are drawing from my knowledge and experience. My wish for you is that you, too, will be able to look back at these hard years with a smile and pride at job well done!

121684